Racing log book

D Maskey

This log book belongs to

Name

Address

Home No:

Mobile No:

Emergency Contact No:

Next of Kin:

Blood Group:

Medical Conditions:

RACE MEETING

_____

Date: _____ Circuit: _____ Class: _____

Organising Club: _____ Championship/Series:

_____ _____

QUALIFYING

Conditions: _____ Tyres Used: _____

Tyre Pressures: Front _____ Rear: _____

Car set up notes: _____

_____

_____

Length on Qualifying: _____ Laps Completed: _____

Fastest Time: _____ On Lap: _____ Position on Grid: _____

Notes on Qualifying

RACE 1

Conditions: _____ Tyres used: _____

Tyre Pressure Front: _____ Rear: _____ Length of Race: _____

Car set up notes: _____

_____

_____

Overall Position:_____Fastest Lap: _____On Lap: _____Position in class: _____

Notes:

_____

RACE 2

Conditions: _____ Tyres used: _____

Tyre Pressure Front: _____ Rear: _____ Length of Race: _____

Car set up notes: _____

_____

_____

Overall Position: _____Fastest Lap: _____On Lap: _____Position in class: _____

Notes:

RACE MEETING

_____

Date: _____ Circuit: _____ Class: _____

Organising Club: _____ Championship/Series:

_____   _____

QUALIFYING

Conditions: _____ Tyres Used: _____

Tyre Pressures: Front _____   Rear: _____

Car set up notes: _____

_____

_____

Length on Qualifying: _____ Laps Completed: _____

Fastest Time: _____ On Lap: _____ Position on Grid: _____

Notes on Qualifying

RACE 1

Conditions: _____ Tyres used: _____

Tyre Pressure Front: _____ Rear: _____ Length of Race: _____

Car set up notes: _____

_____

_____

Overall Position: ____ Fastest Lap: _____ On Lap: _____ Position in class: ____

Notes:

RACE 2

Conditions: _____ Tyres used: _____

Tyre Pressure Front: _____ Rear: _____ Length of Race: _____

Car set up notes: _____

_____

_____

Overall Position: _____ Fastest Lap: _____ On Lap: _____ Position in class: ____

Notes:

RACE MEETING

_____

Date: _____ Circuit: _____ Class: _____

Organising Club: _____ Championship/Series: _____

_____   _____

QUALIFYING

Conditions: _____ Tyres Used: _____

Tyre Pressures: Front _____ Rear: _____

Car set up notes: _____

_____

_____

Length on Qualifying: _____ Laps Completed: _____

Fastest Time: _____ On Lap: _____ Position on Grid: _____

Notes on Qualifying

RACE 1

Conditions: _____ Tyres used: _____

Tyre Pressure Front: _____ Rear: _____ Length of Race: _____

Car set up notes: _____

_____

_____

Overall Position: _____ Fastest Lap: _____ On Lap: _____ Position in class: _____

Notes:

RACE 2

Conditions: _____ Tyres used: _____

Tyre Pressure Front: _____ Rear: _____ Length of Race: _____

Car set up notes: _____

_____

_____

Overall Position: _____ Fastest Lap: _____ On Lap: _____ Position in class: _____

Notes:

RACE MEETING

_____

Date: _____ Circuit: _____ Class: _____

Organising Club: Championship/Series:

_____   _____

QUALIFYING

Conditions: _____ Tyres Used: _____

Tyre Pressures: Front _____   Rear: _____

Car set up notes: _____

_____

_____

Length on Qualifying: _____ Laps Completed: _____

Fastest Time: _____ On Lap: _____ Position on Grid: _____

Notes on Qualifying

RACE 1

Conditions: _____ Tyres used: _____

Tyre Pressure Front: _____ Rear: _____ Length of Race: _____

Car set up notes: _____

_____

_____

Overall Position: _____ Fastest Lap: _____ On Lap: _____ Position in class: _____

Notes:

_____

RACE 2

Conditions: _____ Tyres used: _____

Tyre Pressure Front: _____ Rear: _____ Length of Race: _____

Car set up notes: _____

_____

_____

Overall Position: _____ Fastest Lap: _____ On Lap: _____ Position in class: _____

Notes:

RACE MEETING

_____

Date: _____ Circuit: _____ Class: _____

Organising Club: _____ Championship/Series:

_____ _____

QUALIFYING

Conditions: _____ Tyres Used: _____

Tyre Pressures: Front _____ Rear: _____

Car set up notes: _____

_____

_____

Length on Qualifying: _____ Laps Completed: _____

Fastest Time: _____ On Lap: _____ Position on Grid: _____

Notes on Qualifying

RACE 1

Conditions: _____ Tyres used: _____

Tyre Pressure Front: _____ Rear: _____ Length of Race: _____

Car set up notes: _____

_____

_____

Overall Position: _____ Fastest Lap: _____ On Lap: _____ Position in class: _____

Notes:

RACE 2

Conditions: _____ Tyres used: _____

Tyre Pressure Front: _____ Rear: _____ Length of Race: _____

Car set up notes: _____

_____

_____

Overall Position: _____ Fastest Lap: _____ On Lap: _____ Position in class: _____

Notes:

RACE MEETING

_____

Date: _____ Circuit: _____ Class: _____

Organising Club: Championship/Series:

_____   _____

QUALIFYING

Conditions: _____ Tyres Used: _____

Tyre Pressures: Front _____   Rear: _____

Car set up notes:_____

_____

_____

Length on Qualifying: _____ Laps Completed: _____

Fastest Time: _____ On Lap: _____ Position on Grid: _____

Notes on Qualifying

RACE 1

Conditions: _____ Tyres used: _____

Tyre Pressure Front: _____ Rear: _____ Length of Race: _____

Car set up notes: _____

_____

_____

Overall Position: ____ Fastest Lap: _____ On Lap: _____ Position in class: _____

Notes:

_____

RACE 2

Conditions: _____ Tyres used: _____

Tyre Pressure Front: _____ Rear: _____ Length of Race: _____

Car set up notes: _____

_____

_____

Overall Position: _____ Fastest Lap: _____ On Lap: _____ Position in class: _____

Notes:

RACE MEETING

_____

Date: _____ Circuit: _____ Class: _____

Organising Club: _____ Championship/Series:

_____ _____

QUALIFYING

Conditions: _____ Tyres Used: _____

Tyre Pressures: Front _____ Rear: _____

Car set up notes: _____

_____

_____

Length on Qualifying: _____ Laps Completed: _____

Fastest Time: _____ On Lap: _____ Position on Grid: _____

Notes on Qualifying

RACE 1

Conditions: _____ Tyres used: _____

Tyre Pressure Front: _____ Rear: _____ Length of Race: _____

Car set up notes: _____

_____

_____

Overall Position: _____ Fastest Lap: _____ On Lap: _____ Position in class: _____

Notes:

RACE 2

Conditions: _____ Tyres used: _____

Tyre Pressure Front: _____ Rear: _____ Length of Race: _____

Car set up notes: _____

_____

_____

Overall Position: _____ Fastest Lap: _____ On Lap: _____ Position in class: _____

Notes:

RACE MEETING

_____

Date: _____ Circuit: _____ Class: _____

Organising Club: Championship/Series:

_____   _____

QUALIFYING

Conditions: _____ Tyres Used: _____

Tyre Pressures: Front _____   Rear: _____

Car set up notes: _____

_____

_____

Length on Qualifying: _____ Laps Completed: _____

Fastest Time: _____ On Lap: _____ Position on Grid: _____

Notes on Qualifying

RACE 1

Conditions: _____ Tyres used: _____

Tyre Pressure Front: _____ Rear: _____ Length of Race: _____

Car set up notes: _____

_____

_____

Overall Position: _____ Fastest Lap: _____ On Lap: _____ Position in class: _____

Notes:

_____

RACE 2

Conditions: _____ Tyres used: _____

Tyre Pressure Front: _____ Rear: _____ Length of Race: _____

Car set up notes: _____

_____

_____

Overall Position: _____ Fastest Lap: _____ On Lap: _____ Position in class: _____

Notes:

RACE MEETING

_____

Date: _____ Circuit: _____ Class: _____

Organising Club: _____ Championship/Series: _____

QUALIFYING

Conditions: _____ Tyres Used: _____

Tyre Pressures: Front _____ Rear: _____

Car set up notes: _____

_____

_____

Length on Qualifying: _____ Laps Completed: _____

Fastest Time: _____ On Lap: _____ Position on Grid: _____

Notes on Qualifying

RACE 1

Conditions: _____ Tyres used: _____

Tyre Pressure Front: _____ Rear: _____ Length of Race: _____

Car set up notes: _____

_____

_____

Overall Position: ____ Fastest Lap: _____ On Lap: _____ Position in class: _____

Notes:

RACE 2

Conditions: _____ Tyres used: _____

Tyre Pressure Front: _____ Rear: _____ Length of Race: _____

Car set up notes: _____

_____

_____

Overall Position: _____ Fastest Lap: _____ On Lap: _____ Position in class: _____

Notes:

RACE MEETING

Date: _____ Circuit: _____ Class: _____

Organising Club: _____ Championship/Series: _____

QUALIFYING

Conditions: _____ Tyres Used: _____

Tyre Pressures: Front _____ Rear: _____

Car set up notes: _____

_____

_____

Length on Qualifying: _____ Laps Completed: _____

Fastest Time: _____ On Lap: _____ Position on Grid: _____

Notes on Qualifying

RACE 1

Conditions: _____   Tyres used: _____

Tyre Pressure Front: _____Rear: _____   Length of Race: _____

Car set up notes: _____

_____

_____

Overall Position:____Fastest Lap: _____On Lap: _____Position in class:____

Notes:

RACE 2

Conditions: _____   Tyres used: _____

Tyre Pressure Front: _____Rear: _____   Length of Race: _____

Car set up notes: _____

_____

_____

Overall Position: ____Fastest Lap: _____On Lap: _____Position in class:____

Notes:

RACE MEETING

_____

Date: _____ Circuit: _____ Class: _____

Organising Club: _____ Championship/Series: _____

_____   _____

QUALIFYING

Conditions: _____ Tyres Used: _____

Tyre Pressures: Front _____ Rear: _____

Car set up notes:_____

_____

_____

Length on Qualifying: _____ Laps Completed: _____

Fastest Time: _____ On Lap: _____ Position on Grid: _____

Notes on Qualifying

RACE 1

Conditions: _____ Tyres used: _____

Tyre Pressure Front: _____ Rear: _____ Length of Race: _____

Car set up notes: _____

_____

_____

Overall Position: _____ Fastest Lap: _____ On Lap: _____ Position in class: _____

Notes:

RACE 2

Conditions: _____ Tyres used: _____

Tyre Pressure Front: _____ Rear: _____ Length of Race: _____

Car set up notes: _____

_____

_____

Overall Position: _____ Fastest Lap: _____ On Lap: _____ Position in class: _____

Notes:

RACE MEETING

Date: _____ Circuit: _____ Class: _____

Organising Club: _____ Championship/Series: _____

_____   _____

QUALIFYING

Conditions: _____ Tyres Used: _____

Tyre Pressures: Front _____ Rear: _____

Car set up notes: _____

_____

_____

Length on Qualifying: _____ Laps Completed: _____

Fastest Time: _____ On Lap: _____ Position on Grid: _____

Notes on Qualifying

RACE 1

Conditions: _____ Tyres used: _____

Tyre Pressure Front: _____ Rear: _____ Length of Race: _____

Car set up notes: _____

_____

_____

Overall Position: _____ Fastest Lap: _____ On Lap: _____ Position in class: _____

Notes:

_____

RACE 2

Conditions: _____ Tyres used: _____

Tyre Pressure Front: _____ Rear: _____ Length of Race: _____

Car set up notes: _____

_____

_____

Overall Position: _____ Fastest Lap: _____ On Lap: _____ Position in class: _____

Notes:

RACE MEETING

_____

Date: _____ Circuit: _____ Class: _____

Organising Club: _____ Championship/Series: _____

_____   _____

QUALIFYING

Conditions: _____ Tyres Used: _____

Tyre Pressures: Front _____ Rear: _____

Car set up notes: _____

_____

_____

Length on Qualifying: _____ Laps Completed: _____

Fastest Time: _____ On Lap: _____ Position on Grid: _____

Notes on Qualifying

RACE 1

Conditions: _____ Tyres used: _____

Tyre Pressure Front: _____Rear: _____ Length of Race: _____

Car set up notes: _____

_____

_____

Overall Position:_____Fastest Lap: _____On Lap: _____Position in class: _____

Notes:

_____

RACE 2

Conditions: _____ Tyres used: _____

Tyre Pressure Front: _____Rear: _____ Length of Race: _____

Car set up notes: _____

_____

_____

Overall Position: _____Fastest Lap: _____On Lap: _____Position in class: _____

Notes:

RACE MEETING

_____

Date: _____ Circuit: _____ Class: _____

Organising Club: _____ Championship/Series: _____

QUALIFYING

Conditions: _____ Tyres Used: _____

Tyre Pressures: Front _____ Rear: _____

Car set up notes: _____

_____

_____

Length on Qualifying: _____ Laps Completed: _____

Fastest Time: _____ On Lap: _____ Position on Grid: _____

Notes on Qualifying

RACE 1

Conditions: _____ Tyres used: _____

Tyre Pressure Front: _____ Rear: _____ Length of Race: _____

Car set up notes: _____

_____

_____

Overall Position: _____ Fastest Lap: _____ On Lap: _____ Position in class: _____

Notes:

_____

RACE 2

Conditions: _____ Tyres used: _____

Tyre Pressure Front: _____ Rear: _____ Length of Race: _____

Car set up notes: _____

_____

_____

Overall Position: _____ Fastest Lap: _____ On Lap: _____ Position in class: _____

Notes:

RACE MEETING

_____

Date: _____ Circuit: _____ Class: _____

Organising Club: _____ Championship/Series:

_____ _____

QUALIFYING

Conditions: _____ Tyres Used: _____

Tyre Pressures: Front _____ Rear: _____

Car set up notes: _____

_____

_____

Length on Qualifying: _____ Laps Completed: _____

Fastest Time: _____ On Lap: _____ Position on Grid: _____

Notes on Qualifying

RACE 1

Conditions: _____ Tyres used: _____

Tyre Pressure Front: _____ Rear: _____ Length of Race: _____

Car set up notes: _____

_____

_____

Overall Position: ____ Fastest Lap: _____ On Lap: _____ Position in class: _____

Notes:

_____

RACE 2

Conditions: _____ Tyres used: _____

Tyre Pressure Front: _____ Rear: _____ Length of Race: _____

Car set up notes: _____

_____

_____

Overall Position: _____ Fastest Lap: _____ On Lap: _____ Position in class: _____

Notes:

RACE MEETING

_____

Date: _____ Circuit: _____ Class: _____

Organising Club: _____ Championship/Series: _____

_____ _____

QUALIFYING

Conditions: _____ Tyres Used: _____

Tyre Pressures: Front _____ Rear: _____

Car set up notes: _____

_____

_____

Length on Qualifying: _____ Laps Completed: _____

Fastest Time: _____ On Lap: _____ Position on Grid: _____

Notes on Qualifying

RACE 1

Conditions: _____ Tyres used: _____

Tyre Pressure Front: _____ Rear: _____ Length of Race: _____

Car set up notes: _____

_____

_____

Overall Position: _____ Fastest Lap: _____ On Lap: _____ Position in class: _____

Notes:

RACE 2

Conditions: _____ Tyres used: _____

Tyre Pressure Front: _____ Rear: _____ Length of Race: _____

Car set up notes: _____

_____

_____

Overall Position: _____ Fastest Lap: _____ On Lap: _____ Position in class: _____

Notes:

RACE MEETING

_____

Date: _____ Circuit: _____ Class: _____

Organising Club: _____ Championship/Series: _____

_____   _____

QUALIFYING

Conditions: _____ Tyres Used: _____

Tyre Pressures: Front _____ Rear: _____

Car set up notes: _____

_____

_____

Length on Qualifying: _____ Laps Completed: _____

Fastest Time: _____ On Lap: _____ Position on Grid: _____

Notes on Qualifying

RACE 1

Conditions: _____ Tyres used: _____

Tyre Pressure Front: _____ Rear: _____ Length of Race: _____

Car set up notes: _____

_____

_____

Overall Position: _____ Fastest Lap: _____ On Lap: _____ Position in class: _____

Notes:

RACE 2

Conditions: _____ Tyres used: _____

Tyre Pressure Front: _____ Rear: _____ Length of Race: _____

Car set up notes: _____

_____

_____

Overall Position: _____ Fastest Lap: _____ On Lap: _____ Position in class: _____

Notes:

RACE MEETING

_____

Date: _____ Circuit: _____ Class: _____

Organising Club: _____ Championship/Series: _____

_____   _____

QUALIFYING

Conditions: _____ Tyres Used: _____

Tyre Pressures: Front _____ Rear: _____

Car set up notes: _____

_____

_____

Length on Qualifying: _____ Laps Completed: _____

Fastest Time: _____ On Lap: _____ Position on Grid: _____

Notes on Qualifying

RACE 1

Conditions: _____ Tyres used: _____

Tyre Pressure Front: _____ Rear: _____ Length of Race: _____

Car set up notes: _____

_____

_____

Overall Position: ____ Fastest Lap: _____ On Lap: _____ Position in class: ____

Notes:

RACE 2

Conditions: _____ Tyres used: _____

Tyre Pressure Front: _____ Rear: _____ Length of Race: _____

Car set up notes: _____

_____

_____

Overall Position: ____ Fastest Lap: _____ On Lap: _____ Position in class: ____

Notes:

RACE MEETING

_____

Date: _____ Circuit: _____ Class: _____

Organising Club: Championship/Series:

_____   _____

QUALIFYING

Conditions: _____ Tyres Used: _____

Tyre Pressures: Front _____   Rear: _____

Car set up notes: _____

_____

_____

Length on Qualifying: _____ Laps Completed: _____

Fastest Time: _____ On Lap: _____ Position on Grid: _____

Notes on Qualifying

RACE 1

Conditions: _____ Tyres used: _____

Tyre Pressure Front: _____ Rear: _____ Length of Race: _____

Car set up notes: _____

_____

_____

Overall Position: ____ Fastest Lap: _____ On Lap: _____ Position in class: _____

Notes:

RACE 2

Conditions: _____ Tyres used: _____

Tyre Pressure Front: _____ Rear: _____ Length of Race: _____

Car set up notes: _____

_____

_____

Overall Position: ____ Fastest Lap: _____ On Lap: _____ Position in class: _____

Notes:

RACE MEETING

Date: _____ Circuit: _____ Class: _____

Organising Club: _____ Championship/Series: _____

_____ _____

QUALIFYING

Conditions: _____ Tyres Used: _____

Tyre Pressures: Front _____ Rear: _____

Car set up notes: _____

_____

_____

Length on Qualifying: _____ Laps Completed: _____

Fastest Time: _____ On Lap: _____ Position on Grid: _____

Notes on Qualifying

RACE 1

Conditions: _____ Tyres used: _____

Tyre Pressure Front: _____ Rear: _____ Length of Race: _____

Car set up notes: _____

_____

_____

Overall Position:_____Fastest Lap: _____On Lap: _____Position in class: _____

Notes:

RACE 2

Conditions: _____ Tyres used: _____

Tyre Pressure Front: _____ Rear: _____ Length of Race: _____
Car set up notes: _____

_____

_____

Overall Position: _____Fastest Lap: _____On Lap: _____Position in class: _____

Notes:

RACE MEETING

_____

Date: _____ Circuit: _____ Class: _____

Organising Club: _____ Championship/Series:

_____ _____

QUALIFYING

Conditions: _____ Tyres Used: _____

Tyre Pressures: Front _____ Rear: _____

Car set up notes: _____

_____

_____

Length on Qualifying: _____ Laps Completed: _____

Fastest Time: _____ On Lap: _____ Position on Grid: _____

Notes on Qualifying

RACE 1

Conditions: _____ Tyres used: _____

Tyre Pressure Front: _____ Rear: _____ Length of Race: _____

Car set up notes: _____

_____

_____

Overall Position: _____ Fastest Lap: _____ On Lap: _____ Position in class: _____

Notes:

_____

RACE 2

Conditions: _____ Tyres used: _____

Tyre Pressure Front: _____ Rear: _____ Length of Race: _____

Car set up notes: _____

_____

_____

Overall Position: _____ Fastest Lap: _____ On Lap: _____ Position in class: _____

Notes:

RACE MEETING

_____

Date: _____ Circuit: _____ Class: _____

Organising Club: _____ Championship/Series: _____

_____   _____

QUALIFYING

Conditions: _____ Tyres Used: _____

Tyre Pressures: Front _____   Rear: _____

Car set up notes: _____

_____

_____

Length on Qualifying: _____ Laps Completed: _____

Fastest Time: _____ On Lap: _____ Position on Grid: _____

Notes on Qualifying

RACE 1

Conditions: ———————————— Tyres used: ——————————

Tyre Pressure Front: ————— Rear: ——————— Length of Race: —————

Car set up notes: ——————————————————————————————————

——

——

Overall Position:———Fastest Lap: ——————On Lap: ————Position in class: ————

Notes:

RACE 2

Conditions: ——————————————— Tyres used: ——————————

Tyre Pressure Front: ————— Rear: ——————— Length of Race: —————

Car set up notes:

——

——

Overall Position: ————Fastest Lap: ——————On Lap: ————Position in class: ————

Notes:

RACE MEETING

_____

Date: _____ Circuit: _____ Class: _____

Organising Club: _____ Championship/Series:

_____ _____

QUALIFYING

Conditions: _____ Tyres Used: _____

Tyre Pressures: Front _____ Rear: _____

Car set up notes: _____

_____

_____

Length on Qualifying: _____ Laps Completed: _____

Fastest Time: _____ On Lap: _____ Position on Grid: _____

Notes on Qualifying

RACE 1

Conditions: _____ Tyres used: _____

Tyre Pressure Front: _____ Rear: _____ Length of Race: _____

Car set up notes: _____

_____

_____

Overall Position: _____ Fastest Lap: _____ On Lap: _____ Position in class: _____

Notes:

_____

RACE 2

Conditions: _____ Tyres used: _____

Tyre Pressure Front: _____ Rear: _____ Length of Race: _____

Car set up notes: _____

_____

_____

Overall Position: _____ Fastest Lap: _____ On Lap: _____ Position in class: _____

Notes:

RACE MEETING

_____

Date: _____ Circuit: _____ Class: _____

Organising Club: _____ Championship/Series:

_____ _____

QUALIFYING

Conditions: _____ Tyres Used: _____

Tyre Pressures: Front _____ Rear: _____

Car set up notes: _____

_____

_____

Length on Qualifying: _____ Laps Completed: _____

Fastest Time: _____ On Lap: _____ Position on Grid: _____

Notes on Qualifying

RACE 1

Conditions: _____ Tyres used: _____

Tyre Pressure Front: _____ Rear: _____ Length of Race: _____

Car set up notes: _____

_____

_____

Overall Position: ____ Fastest Lap: _____ On Lap: _____ Position in class: _____

Notes:

_____

RACE 2

Conditions: _____ Tyres used: _____

Tyre Pressure Front: _____ Rear: _____ Length of Race: _____

Car set up notes: _____

_____

_____

Overall Position: _____ Fastest Lap: _____ On Lap: _____ Position in class: _____

Notes:

RACE MEETING

_____

Date: _____ Circuit: _____ Class: _____

Organising Club: _____ Championship/Series: _____

_____ _____

QUALIFYING

Conditions: _____ Tyres Used: _____

Tyre Pressures: Front _____ Rear: _____

Car set up notes: _____

_____

_____

Length on Qualifying: _____ Laps Completed: _____

Fastest Time: _____ On Lap: _____ Position on Grid: _____

Notes on Qualifying

RACE 1

Conditions: _____ Tyres used: _____

Tyre Pressure Front: _____ Rear: _____ Length of Race: _____

Car set up notes: _____

_____

_____

Overall Position: _____ Fastest Lap: _____ On Lap: _____ Position in class: _____

Notes:

RACE 2

Conditions: _____ Tyres used: _____

Tyre Pressure Front: _____ Rear: _____ Length of Race: _____

Car set up notes: _____

_____

_____

Overall Position: _____ Fastest Lap: _____ On Lap: _____ Position in class: _____

Notes:

RACE MEETING

_____

Date: _____ Circuit: _____ Class: _____

Organising Club: _____ Championship/Series: _____

_____   _____

QUALIFYING

Conditions: _____ Tyres Used: _____

Tyre Pressures: Front _____   Rear: _____

Car set up notes: _____

_____

_____

Length on Qualifying: _____ Laps Completed: _____

Fastest Time: _____ On Lap: _____ Position on Grid: _____

Notes on Qualifying

RACE 1

Conditions: _____ Tyres used: _____

Tyre Pressure Front: _____ Rear: _____ Length of Race: _____

Car set up notes: _____

_____

_____

Overall Position:____Fastest Lap: _____On Lap: _____Position in class: ____

Notes:

RACE 2

Conditions: _____ Tyres used: _____

Tyre Pressure Front: _____ Rear: _____ Length of Race: _____

Car set up notes: _____

_____

_____

Overall Position: ____Fastest Lap: _____On Lap: _____Position in class: ____

Notes:

RACE MEETING

_____

Date: _____ Circuit: _____ Class: _____

Organising Club: _____ Championship/Series: _____

_____   _____

QUALIFYING

Conditions: _____ Tyres Used: _____

Tyre Pressures: Front _____ Rear: _____

Car set up notes: _____

_____

_____

Length on Qualifying: _____ Laps Completed: _____

Fastest Time: _____ On Lap: _____ Position on Grid: _____

Notes on Qualifying

RACE 1

Conditions: _____ Tyres used: _____

Tyre Pressure Front: _____ Rear: _____ Length of Race: _____

Car set up notes: _____

_____

_____

Overall Position: _____ Fastest Lap: _____ On Lap: _____ Position in class: _____

Notes:

_____

RACE 2

Conditions: _____ Tyres used: _____

Tyre Pressure Front: _____ Rear: _____ Length of Race: _____

Car set up notes: _____

_____

_____

Overall Position: _____ Fastest Lap: _____ On Lap: _____ Position in class: _____

Notes:

RACE MEETING

_____

Date: _____ Circuit: _____ Class: _____

Organising Club: Championship/Series:

_____   _____

QUALIFYING

Conditions: _____ Tyres Used: _____

Tyre Pressures: Front _____   Rear: _____

Car set up notes:_____

_____

_____

Length on Qualifying: _____ Laps Completed: _____

Fastest Time: _____ On Lap: _____ Position on Grid: _____

Notes on Qualifying

RACE 1

Conditions: _____ Tyres used: _____

Tyre Pressure Front: _____ Rear: _____ Length of Race: _____

Car set up notes: _____

_____

_____

Overall Position: ____ Fastest Lap: ____ On Lap: ____ Position in class: ____

Notes:

RACE 2

Conditions: _____ Tyres used: _____

Tyre Pressure Front: _____ Rear: _____ Length of Race: _____

Car set up notes: _____

_____

_____

Overall Position: ____ Fastest Lap: ____ On Lap: ____ Position in class: ____

Notes:

RACE MEETING

_____

Date: _____ Circuit: _____ Class: _____

Organising Club: _____ Championship/Series:

_____ _____

QUALIFYING

Conditions: _____ Tyres Used: _____

Tyre Pressures: Front _____ Rear: _____

Car set up notes: _____

_____

_____

Length on Qualifying: _____ Laps Completed: _____

Fastest Time: _____ On Lap: _____ Position on Grid: _____

Notes on Qualifying

RACE 1

Conditions: _____ Tyres used: _____

Tyre Pressure Front: _____ Rear: _____ Length of Race: _____

Car set up notes: _____

_____

_____

Overall Position: ____ Fastest Lap: _____ On Lap: _____ Position in class: ____

Notes:

RACE 2

Conditions: _____ Tyres used: _____

Tyre Pressure Front: _____ Rear: _____ Length of Race: _____

Car set up notes: _____

_____

_____

Overall Position: _____ Fastest Lap: _____ On Lap: _____ Position in class: ____

Notes:

RACE MEETING

_____

Date: _____ Circuit: _____ Class: _____

Organising Club: _____ Championship/Series:

_____ _____

QUALIFYING

Conditions: _____ Tyres Used: _____

Tyre Pressures: Front _____ Rear: _____

Car set up notes: _____

_____

_____

Length on Qualifying: _____ Laps Completed: _____

Fastest Time: _____ On Lap: _____ Position on Grid: _____

Notes on Qualifying

RACE 1

Conditions: _____ Tyres used: _____

Tyre Pressure Front: _____Rear: _____ Length of Race: _____

Car set up notes: _____

_____

_____

Overall Position:_____Fastest Lap: _____On Lap: _____Position in class: _____

Notes:

_____

RACE 2

Conditions: _____ Tyres used: _____

Tyre Pressure Front: _____Rear: _____ Length of Race: _____

Car set up notes: _____

_____

_____

Overall Position: _____Fastest Lap: _____On Lap: _____Position in class: _____

Notes:

RACE MEETING

_____

Date: _____ Circuit: _____ Class: _____

Organising Club: _____ Championship/Series:

_____ _____

QUALIFYING

Conditions: _____ Tyres Used: _____

Tyre Pressures: Front _____ Rear: _____

Car set up notes: _____

_____

_____

Length on Qualifying: _____ Laps Completed: _____

Fastest Time: _____ On Lap: _____ Position on Grid: _____

Notes on Qualifying

RACE 1

Conditions: _____ Tyres used: _____

Tyre Pressure Front: _____ Rear: _____ Length of Race: _____

Car set up notes: _____

_____

_____

Overall Position: _____ Fastest Lap: _____ On Lap: _____ Position in class: _____

Notes:

RACE 2

Conditions: _____ Tyres used: _____

Tyre Pressure Front: _____ Rear: _____ Length of Race: _____

Car set up notes: _____

_____

_____

Overall Position: _____ Fastest Lap: _____ On Lap: _____ Position in class: _____

Notes:

RACE MEETING

_____

Date: _____ Circuit: _____ Class: _____

Organising Club: Championship/Series:

_____   _____

QUALIFYING

Conditions: _____ Tyres Used: _____

Tyre Pressures: Front _____   Rear: _____

Car set up notes: _____

_____

_____

Length on Qualifying: _____ Laps Completed: _____

Fastest Time: _____ On Lap: _____ Position on Grid: _____

Notes on Qualifying

RACE 1

Conditions: _____ Tyres used: _____

Tyre Pressure Front: _____ Rear: _____ Length of Race: _____

Car set up notes: _____

_____

_____

Overall Position: _____ Fastest Lap: _____ On Lap: _____ Position in class: _____

Notes:

_____

RACE 2

Conditions: _____ Tyres used: _____

Tyre Pressure Front: _____ Rear: _____ Length of Race: _____

Car set up notes: _____

_____

_____

Overall Position: _____ Fastest Lap: _____ On Lap: _____ Position in class: _____

Notes:

RACE MEETING

_____

Date: _____ Circuit: _____ Class: _____

Organising Club: _____ Championship/Series: _____

_____ _____

QUALIFYING

Conditions: _____ Tyres Used: _____

Tyre Pressures: Front _____ Rear: _____

Car set up notes: _____

_____

_____

Length on Qualifying: _____ Laps Completed: _____

Fastest Time: _____ On Lap: _____ Position on Grid: _____

Notes on Qualifying

RACE 1

Conditions: _____ Tyres used: _____

Tyre Pressure Front: _____ Rear: _____ Length of Race: _____

Car set up notes: _____

_____

_____

Overall Position: _____ Fastest Lap: _____ On Lap: _____ Position in class: _____

Notes:

_____

RACE 2

Conditions: _____ Tyres used: _____

Tyre Pressure Front: _____ Rear: _____ Length of Race: _____

Car set up notes: _____

_____

_____

Overall Position: _____ Fastest Lap: _____ On Lap: _____ Position in class: _____

Notes:

RACE MEETING

_____

Date: _____ Circuit: _____ Class: _____

Organising Club: _____ Championship/Series: _____

_____ _____

QUALIFYING

Conditions: _____ Tyres Used: _____

Tyre Pressures: Front _____ Rear: _____

Car set up notes:_____

_____

_____

Length on Qualifying: _____ Laps Completed: _____

Fastest Time: _____ On Lap: _____ Position on Grid: _____

Notes on Qualifying

RACE 1

Conditions: _____ Tyres used: _____

Tyre Pressure Front: _____ Rear: _____ Length of Race: _____

Car set up notes: _____

_____

_____

Overall Position: ____ Fastest Lap: _____ On Lap: _____ Position in class: _____

Notes:

_____

RACE 2

Conditions: _____ Tyres used: _____

Tyre Pressure Front: _____ Rear: _____ Length of Race: _____

Car set up notes: _____

_____

_____

Overall Position: _____ Fastest Lap: _____ On Lap: _____ Position in class: ___

Notes:

RACE MEETING

_____

Date: _____ Circuit: _____ Class: _____

Organising Club: _____ Championship/Series:

_____ _____

QUALIFYING

Conditions: _____ Tyres Used: _____

Tyre Pressures: Front _____ Rear: _____

Car set up notes: _____

_____

_____

Length on Qualifying: _____ Laps Completed: _____

Fastest Time: _____ On Lap: _____ Position on Grid: _____

Notes on Qualifying

RACE 1

Conditions: _____ Tyres used: _____

Tyre Pressure Front: _____ Rear: _____ Length of Race: _____

Car set up notes: _____

_____

_____

Overall Position: _____ Fastest Lap: _____ On Lap: _____ Position in class: _____

Notes:

_____

RACE 2

Conditions: _____ Tyres used: _____

Tyre Pressure Front: _____ Rear: _____ Length of Race: _____

Car set up notes: _____

_____

_____

Overall Position: _____ Fastest Lap: _____ On Lap: _____ Position in class: _____

Notes:

RACE MEETING

Date: _____ Circuit: _____ Class: _____

Organising Club: _____ Championship/Series: _____

QUALIFYING

Conditions: _____ Tyres Used: _____

Tyre Pressures: Front _____   Rear: _____

Car set up notes: _____

_____

_____

Length on Qualifying: _____ Laps Completed: _____

Fastest Time: _____ On Lap: _____ Position on Grid: _____

Notes on Qualifying

RACE 1

Conditions: _____ Tyres used: _____

Tyre Pressure Front: _____ Rear: _____ Length of Race: _____

Car set up notes: _____

_____

_____

Overall Position: _____ Fastest Lap: _____ On Lap: _____ Position in class: _____

Notes:

_____

RACE 2

Conditions: _____ Tyres used: _____

Tyre Pressure Front: _____ Rear: _____ Length of Race: _____

Car set up notes: _____

_____

_____

Overall Position: _____ Fastest Lap: _____ On Lap: _____ Position in class: _____

Notes:

RACE MEETING

_____

Date: _____ Circuit: _____ Class: _____

Organising Club: _____ Championship/Series:

_____ _____

QUALIFYING

Conditions: _____ Tyres Used: _____

Tyre Pressures: Front _____ Rear: _____

Car set up notes: _____

_____

_____

Length on Qualifying: _____ Laps Completed: _____

Fastest Time: _____ On Lap: _____ Position on Grid: _____

Notes on Qualifying

RACE 1

Conditions: _____ Tyres used: _____

Tyre Pressure Front: _____ Rear: _____ Length of Race: _____

Car set up notes: _____

_____

_____

Overall Position: _____ Fastest Lap: _____ On Lap: _____ Position in class: _____

Notes:

RACE 2

Conditions: _____ Tyres used: _____

Tyre Pressure Front: _____ Rear: _____ Length of Race: _____

Car set up notes: _____

_____

_____

Overall Position: _____ Fastest Lap: _____ On Lap: _____ Position in class: _____

Notes:

RACE MEETING

_____

Date: _____ Circuit: _____ Class: _____

Organising Club: _____ Championship/Series: _____

_____   _____

QUALIFYING

Conditions: _____ Tyres Used: _____

Tyre Pressures: Front _____ Rear: _____

Car set up notes: _____

_____

_____

Length on Qualifying: _____ Laps Completed: _____

Fastest Time: _____ On Lap: _____ Position on Grid: _____

Notes on Qualifying

RACE 1

Conditions: _____ Tyres used: _____

Tyre Pressure Front: _____ Rear: _____ Length of Race: _____

Car set up notes: _____

_____

_____

Overall Position:_____Fastest Lap: _____On Lap: _____Position in class: _____

Notes:

RACE 2

Conditions: _____ Tyres used: _____

Tyre Pressure Front: _____ Rear: _____ Length of Race: _____

Car set up notes: _____

_____

_____

Overall Position: _____Fastest Lap: _____On Lap: _____Position in class: _____

Notes:

RACE MEETING

_____

Date: _____ Circuit: _____ Class: _____

Organising Club: _____ Championship/Series: _____

_____ _____

QUALIFYING

Conditions: _____ Tyres Used: _____

Tyre Pressures: Front _____ Rear: _____

Car set up notes: _____

_____

_____

Length on Qualifying: _____ Laps Completed: _____

Fastest Time: _____ On Lap: _____ Position on Grid: _____

Notes on Qualifying

RACE 1

Conditions: _____ Tyres used: _____

Tyre Pressure Front: _____ Rear: _____ Length of Race: _____

Car set up notes: _____

_____

_____

Overall Position: ____ Fastest Lap: _____ On Lap: ____ Position in class: ____

Notes:

_____

RACE 2

Conditions: _____ Tyres used: _____

Tyre Pressure Front: _____ Rear: _____ Length of Race: _____

Car set up notes: _____

_____

_____

Overall Position: ____ Fastest Lap: _____ On Lap: ____ Position in class: ____

Notes:

RACE MEETING

_____

Date: _____ Circuit: _____ Class: _____

Organising Club: _____ Championship/Series:

_____ _____

QUALIFYING

Conditions: _____ Tyres Used: _____

Tyre Pressures: Front _____ Rear: _____

Car set up notes:_____

_____

_____

Length on Qualifying: _____ Laps Completed: _____

Fastest Time: _____ On Lap: _____ Position on Grid: _____

Notes on Qualifying

RACE 1

Conditions: _____ Tyres used: _____

Tyre Pressure Front: _____Rear: _____ Length of Race: _____

Car set up notes: _____

_____

_____

Overall Position:____Fastest Lap: _____On Lap: ____Position in class: ____

Notes:

_____

RACE 2

Conditions: _____ Tyres used: _____

Tyre Pressure Front: _____Rear: _____ Length of Race: _____

Car set up notes: _____

_____

_____

Overall Position: ____Fastest Lap: _____On Lap: ____Position in class: ____

Notes:

RACE MEETING

_____

Date: _____ Circuit: _____ Class: _____

Organising Club: _____ Championship/Series:

_____   _____

QUALIFYING

Conditions: _____ Tyres Used: _____

Tyre Pressures: Front _____ Rear: _____

Car set up notes: _____

_____

_____

Length on Qualifying: _____ Laps Completed: _____

Fastest Time: _____ On Lap: _____ Position on Grid: _____

Notes on Qualifying

RACE 1

Conditions: _____ Tyres used: _____

Tyre Pressure Front: _____Rear: _____ Length of Race: _____

Car set up notes: _____

_____

_____

Overall Position:____Fastest Lap: _____On Lap: ____Position in class: ____

Notes:

RACE 2

Conditions: _____ Tyres used: _____

Tyre Pressure Front: _____Rear: _____ Length of Race: _____

Car set up notes: _____

_____

_____

Overall Position: ____Fastest Lap: _____On Lap: ____Position in class: ____

Notes:

RACE MEETING

_____

Date: _____ Circuit: _____ Class: _____

Organising Club: _____ Championship/Series: _____

_____   _____

QUALIFYING

Conditions: _____ Tyres Used: _____

Tyre Pressures: Front _____ Rear: _____

Car set up notes: _____

_____

_____

Length on Qualifying: _____ Laps Completed: _____

Fastest Time: _____ On Lap: _____ Position on Grid: _____

Notes on Qualifying

RACE 1

Conditions: _____ Tyres used: _____

Tyre Pressure Front: _____ Rear: _____ Length of Race: _____

Car set up notes: _____

_____

_____

Overall Position: ____ Fastest Lap: _____ On Lap: ____ Position in class: ____

Notes:

_____

RACE 2

Conditions: _____ Tyres used: _____

Tyre Pressure Front: _____ Rear: _____ Length of Race: _____

Car set up notes: _____

_____

_____

Overall Position: ____ Fastest Lap: _____ On Lap: ____ Position in class: ____

Notes:

RACE MEETING

_____

Date: _____ Circuit: _____ Class: _____

Organising Club: _____ Championship/Series: _____

_____   _____

QUALIFYING

Conditions: _____ Tyres Used: _____

Tyre Pressures: Front _____ Rear: _____

Car set up notes: _____

_____

_____

Length on Qualifying: _____ Laps Completed: _____

Fastest Time: _____ On Lap: _____ Position on Grid: _____

Notes on Qualifying

RACE 1

Conditions: _____ Tyres used: _____

Tyre Pressure Front: _____ Rear: _____ Length of Race: _____

Car set up notes: _____

_____

_____

Overall Position: _____ Fastest Lap: _____ On Lap: _____ Position in class: _____

Notes:

_____

RACE 2

Conditions: _____ Tyres used: _____

Tyre Pressure Front: _____ Rear: _____ Length of Race: _____

Car set up notes: _____

_____

_____

Overall Position: _____ Fastest Lap: _____ On Lap: _____ Position in class: _____

Notes:

RACE MEETING

_____

Date: _____ Circuit: _____ Class: _____

Organising Club: _____ Championship/Series: _____

_____ _____

QUALIFYING

Conditions: _____ Tyres Used: _____

Tyre Pressures: Front _____ Rear: _____

Car set up notes: _____

_____

_____

Length on Qualifying: _____ Laps Completed: _____

Fastest Time: _____ On Lap: _____ Position on Grid: _____

Notes on Qualifying

RACE 1

Conditions: _____ Tyres used: _____

Tyre Pressure Front: _____ Rear: _____ Length of Race: _____

Car set up notes: _____

_____

_____

Overall Position: _____ Fastest Lap: _____ On Lap: _____ Position in class: _____

Notes:

RACE 2

Conditions: _____ Tyres used: _____

Tyre Pressure Front: _____ Rear: _____ Length of Race: _____

Car set up notes: _____

_____

_____

Overall Position: _____ Fastest Lap: _____ On Lap: _____ Position in class: _____

Notes:

RACE MEETING

_____

Date: _____ Circuit: _____ Class: _____

Organising Club: _____ Championship/Series: _____

_____   _____

QUALIFYING

Conditions: _____ Tyres Used: _____

Tyre Pressures: Front _____ Rear: _____

Car set up notes: _____

_____

_____

Length on Qualifying: _____ Laps Completed: _____

Fastest Time: _____ On Lap: _____ Position on Grid: _____

Notes on Qualifying

RACE 1

Conditions: _____   Tyres used: _____

Tyre Pressure Front: _____ Rear: _____   Length of Race: _____

Car set up notes: _____

_____

_____

Overall Position: _____ Fastest Lap: _____ On Lap: _____ Position in class: _____

Notes:

RACE 2

Conditions: _____   Tyres used: _____

Tyre Pressure Front: _____ Rear: _____   Length of Race: _____

Car set up notes: _____

_____

_____

Overall Position: _____ Fastest Lap: _____ On Lap: _____ Position in class: _____

Notes:

RACE MEETING

_____

Date: _____ Circuit: _____ Class: _____

Organising Club: _____ Championship/Series:

_____ _____

QUALIFYING

Conditions: _____ Tyres Used: _____

Tyre Pressures: Front _____ Rear: _____

Car set up notes: _____

_____

_____

Length on Qualifying: _____ Laps Completed: _____

Fastest Time: _____ On Lap: _____ Position on Grid: _____

Notes on Qualifying

RACE 1

Conditions: _____ Tyres used: _____

Tyre Pressure Front: _____Rear: _____ Length of Race: _____

Car set up notes: _____

_____

_____

Overall Position:____Fastest Lap: _____On Lap: _____Position in class: _____

Notes:

RACE 2

Conditions: _____ Tyres used: _____

Tyre Pressure Front: _____Rear: _____ Length of Race: _____
Car set up notes: _____

_____

_____

Overall Position: _____Fastest Lap: _____On Lap: _____Position in class: ___

Notes:

RACE MEETING

_____

Date: _____ Circuit: _____ Class: _____

Organising Club: _____ Championship/Series: _____

_____

QUALIFYING

Conditions: _____ Tyres Used: _____

Tyre Pressures: Front _____ Rear: _____

Car set up notes: _____

_____

_____

Length on Qualifying: _____ Laps Completed: _____

Fastest Time: _____ On Lap: _____ Position on Grid: _____

Notes on Qualifying

RACE 1

Conditions: _____ Tyres used: _____

Tyre Pressure Front: _____ Rear: _____ Length of Race: _____

Car set up notes: _____

_____

_____

Overall Position: ____ Fastest Lap: _____ On Lap: _____ Position in class: ____

Notes:

_____

RACE 2

Conditions: _____ Tyres used: _____

Tyre Pressure Front: _____ Rear: _____ Length of Race: _____

Car set up notes: _____

_____

_____

Overall Position: ____ Fastest Lap: _____ On Lap: _____ Position in class: ____

Notes:

RACE MEETING

_____

Date: _____ Circuit: _____ Class: _____

Organising Club: Championship/Series:

_____   _____

QUALIFYING

Conditions: _____ Tyres Used: _____

Tyre Pressures: Front _____   Rear: _____

Car set up notes: _____

_____

_____

Length on Qualifying: _____ Laps Completed: _____

Fastest Time: _____ On Lap: _____ Position on Grid: _____

Notes on Qualifying

RACE 1

Conditions: _____ Tyres used: _____

Tyre Pressure Front: _____ Rear: _____ Length of Race: _____

Car set up notes: _____

_____

_____

Overall Position:____Fastest Lap: _____On Lap: _____Position in class: ____

Notes:

RACE 2

Conditions: _____ Tyres used: _____

Tyre Pressure Front: _____Rear: _____ Length of Race: _____

Car set up notes: _____

_____

_____

Overall Position: ____Fastest Lap: _____On Lap: _____Position in class: ____

Notes:

RACE MEETING

_____

Date: _____ Circuit: _____ Class: _____

Organising Club: _____ Championship/Series:

_____   _____

QUALIFYING

Conditions: _____ Tyres Used: _____

Tyre Pressures: Front _____ Rear: _____

Car set up notes: _____

_____

_____

Length on Qualifying: _____ Laps Completed: _____

Fastest Time: _____ On Lap: _____ Position on Grid: _____

Notes on Qualifying

Printed in Great Britain
by Amazon

12605526R00059